Florida

by Sandra J. Christian, M. Ed.

Consultant:
David McCally, Ph.D.
Professor
Department of History
University of Florida
Gainesville, Florida

Capstone press
Mankato, Minnesota

Capstone Press
151 Good Counsel Drive • P.O. Box 669 • Mankato, Minnesota 56002
http://www.capstone-press.com

Library of Congress Cataloging-in-Publication Data
Christian, Sandra J.
    Florida/by Sandra J. Christian.
    v. cm.—(Land of liberty)
    Includes bibliographical references and index.
    Contents: About Florida—Land, climate, and wildlife—History of Florida—
Government and politics—Economy and resources—People and culture.
    ISBN 0-7368-1577-5 (hardcover)
    1. Florida—Juvenile literature. [1. Florida.] I. Title. II. Series.
F311.3.C475 2003
975.9—dc21   2002011787

Summary: An introduction to the geography, history, government, politics,
economy, resources, people, and culture of Florida, including maps, charts,
and a recipe.

Editorial Credits
Kremena Spengler, editor; Jennifer Schonborn, series and book designer; Angi
Gahler, illustrator; Kelly Garvin, photo researcher; Eric Kudalis, product
planning editor

Photo Credits

Cover images: aerial view of Miami Beach, PhotoDisc, Inc.; alligator in
Loxahatchee National Wildlife Refuge, James P. Rowan

Capstone Press/Gary Sundermeyer, 54; Corbis/Bettmann, 27, 28; Corbis/Najlah
Feanny, 15; Corbis/NASA/Roger Ressmeyer, 4; Corbis/Raymond Gehman, 34;
Digital Stock, 1, 56; Getty Images, 53; Houserstock/Dave G. Houser, 17, 32, 44,
50-51; Houserstock/Jan Butchofsky, 18, 46; Houserstock/Michael J. Pettypool, 8;
Hulton Archive by Getty Images, 30-31, 39; James P. Rowan, 16, 40, 57; North
Wind Picture Archives, 20, 23, 24, 58; Tom Till, 12-13, 63; One Mile Up, Inc.,
55 (both); U.S. Postal Service, 59; William H. Allen Jr., 42-43

Artistic Effects
Digital Stock, PhotoDisc, Inc., Visit Florida

1 2 3 4 5 6 08 07 06 05 04 03

Table of Contents

Space shuttles launch from Cape Canaveral in eastern Florida.

Chapter 1

About Florida

For more than 40 years, rockets and space shuttles have blasted off from Cape Canaveral on Florida's Atlantic coast. The first U.S. astronaut, Alan Shepard, lifted off from Cape Canaveral in 1961. The Hubble Telescope and the International Space Station also launched from Florida.

The Kennedy Space Center on Cape Canaveral tells the story of the U.S. space program. Visitors can see real rockets. They can meet with an astronaut and watch live broadcasts from present missions. Live shuttle launches can be seen from a 60-foot (18-meter) tall observation tower. A full-sized model of the shuttle *Explorer* shows where shuttle crews work, sleep, and eat. Guests can even enter their names in a drawing to fly into space in the future.

The Sunshine State

From space rockets to sunny beaches, Florida is an exciting state. Water sports fans swim, sail, fish, and snorkel in the warm ocean off the Florida coast. Beach lovers explore the sandy coastline lined with palm trees. Families on vacation crowd into roller coasters in Florida's theme parks. Some nature lovers look for alligators and water birds in the marshes, swamps, and rivers. Others explore south Florida's living coral reefs and other ocean life.

Florida forms the southeastern tip of the United States. Alabama and Georgia border it on the north. The Atlantic Ocean lies to its east, and the Gulf of Mexico to its west. Hawaii is the only state located farther south than Florida. Florida's year-round sunny climate gives it the nickname "The Sunshine State."

Florida Cities

ALABAMA

GEORGIA

ATLANTIC OCEAN

⭐ Tallahassee

Pensacola

Jacksonville

St. Augustine

Gainesville

Ocala

Daytona Beach

Gulf of Mexico

Orlando

Cape Canaveral

Tampa

St. Petersburg

FLORIDA

West Palm Beach

Fort Myers

Fort Lauderdale

Miami

Florida Keys

Key West

N
W   E
S

Legend

	American Indian Reservation
⭐	Capital
●	City

Scale

Miles
0   40   80   120

0   40   80   120   160
Kilometers

Millions of years ago, wind and water shaped Florida's beaches.

Chapter 2

Land, Climate, and Wildlife

The Florida peninsula is a long, narrow piece of land. But what people see is only the top of a much larger landform. If the sea level were just 300 feet (91 meters) lower, the Florida peninsula would be much wider.

The peninsula formed over millions of years. When icebergs melted, the sea level rose. Sometimes, the sea covered the peninsula entirely. When the sea level fell, the land showed above the ocean.

These changes helped shape Florida's land. When the land was underwater, new rock layers formed from the shells of dead sea animals. These limestone layers formed Florida's flat surface. As the land appeared above the sea, wind and rain created river valleys and large, shifting piles of sand called dunes. Waves shaped the beaches, bays, and sandy islands that make up Florida's coastline. Florida's coastline stretches for 1,350 miles (2,173 kilometers). Only Alaska's coastline is longer.

Florida is divided into five land regions. They are the Central Highlands, Northern Highlands, Coastal Lowlands, Marianna Lowlands, and the Southern Zone.

Highlands and Lowlands

Although Florida is basically flat, it does have marked highlands and lowlands. The Central Highlands form the middle of the peninsula. The Northern Highlands stretch into the Florida Panhandle. The Panhandle is an area in northwest Florida shaped like the handle of a frying pan. The Central and Northern Highlands are covered with lakes, rivers, and springs. In some places, the ground forms bowl-like depressions called sinkholes. Sinkholes form when water washes away the soft limestone layer under the soil.

Florida's Land Features

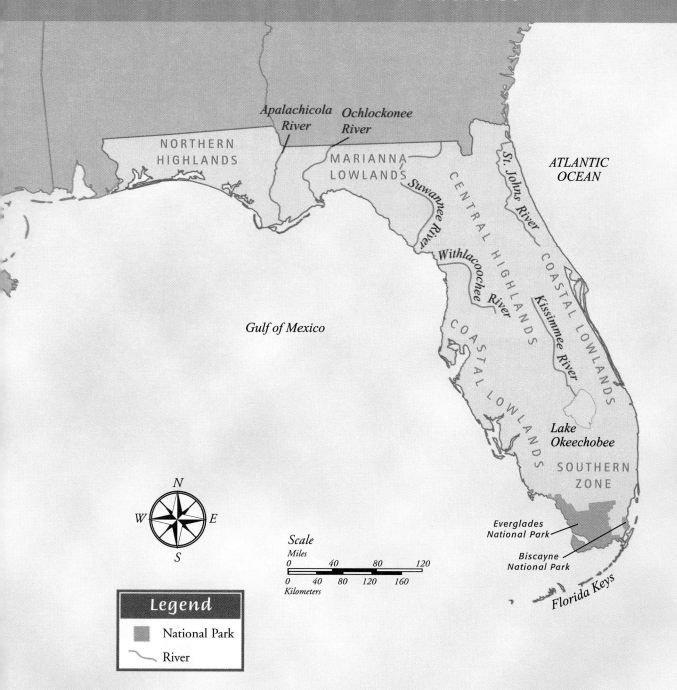

Apalachicola River

Ochlockonee River

NORTHERN HIGHLANDS

MARIANNA LOWLANDS

Suwannee River

CENTRAL HIGHLANDS

St. Johns River

ATLANTIC OCEAN

Withlacoochee River

COASTAL LOWLANDS

Kissimmee River

Gulf of Mexico

COASTAL LOWLANDS

Lake Okeechobee

SOUTHERN ZONE

N
W E
S

Scale
Miles
0   40   80   120
0 40 80 120 160
Kilometers

Everglades National Park

Biscayne National Park

Florida Keys

Legend

National Park

River

The Coastal Lowlands form the rim of the Florida peninsula. Most of the coastline is sandy, with dunes formed by blowing winds.

The Marianna Lowlands are in north-central Florida. This area has low, rolling hills with rivers and streams.

The Southern Zone

The Everglades, Big Cypress Swamp, and Lake Okeechobee form a large wetland area in southern Florida. Grass-covered

marshes and tree-covered swamps make up most of this region. The Everglades is actually a slow-flowing river covered with water grasses. On average, the Everglades is 40 miles (64 kilometers) wide and just 6 inches (15 centimeters) deep. Lake Okeechobee is Florida's largest lake. It is 730 square miles (1,891 square kilometers) wide and 6 to 10 feet (1.8 to 3 meters) deep.

The Florida Keys lie just south of Florida's southern tip. This chain of about 3,000 small islands stretches more than

Marsh grasses cover much of the Everglades in southern Florida.

150 miles (240 kilometers). The islands are coral reefs that lie on a thick layer of limestone. A road links the islands to the Florida peninsula and to each other.

Climate

The water and land near Florida affect the state's climate. The Gulf of Mexico and the Caribbean Sea make the climate warm and humid during most of the year. In late fall, winter, and early spring, winds from the north quickly cool Florida's temperatures.

In most of Florida, a cool, dry winter follows a warm, rainy summer. During the dry season, temperatures can fall below freezing. Frosts have killed plants and forced farmers to move citrus groves farther south. During the wet season, storms from the Atlantic and Caribbean bring heavy rains to Florida. These storms can become hurricanes that cause flooding, property damage, and human deaths.

Because of its length, Florida spans different climate zones. The climate of Key West is different from the rest of Florida. Weather scientists describe the hot climate of Key West as tropical.

Hurricanes

Florida experiences large wind and rain storms called hurricanes. The National Weather Service names these storms to make it easier for weathercasters to give weather warnings.

Hurricanes form over the ocean in late summer and fall. Winds of more than 150 miles (240 kilometers) per hour and heavy rains can cause flooding and storm surges. Storm surges are large amounts of water from the ocean that crash into the coast.

Hurricane Andrew hit southern Florida on August 24, 1992. It caused 58 deaths. The hurricane destroyed 25,000 homes, including the ones at left, and damaged 10,000 others. It cost $20 billion to rebuild after Hurricane Andrew.

Plants and Animals

Florida's humid climate supports a variety of animals and plants. More plants, birds, and snakes live in Florida than in any other state east of the Mississippi River. Most other parts of the world at the same latitude are deserts. The oceans around Florida add moisture to the air. The moisture helps animals and plants survive.

The inner peninsula is rich in plant and animal life. Pines and oaks grow in the uplands. The wooded areas are home to gray foxes, wildcats, and black bears. Water lilies and saw grass

The common egret and other wading birds live in Florida's wetlands.

Red mangroves grow out of the salty water along the Florida coast.

grow in the marshes. Cypress, cedar, and palm trees rise above the swamps. Herons, egrets, ibis, and flamingos nest in these wetlands. Freshwater lakes are home to bass and crappies.

Mangrove trees grow out of the water along Florida's southern coast. The trees' shallow roots allow them to grow well in wet soil. Some varieties even drop roots from branches and upper parts of their trunks. These roots make the trees look twisted.

The water around Florida is filled with animals. Crabs, crayfish, and oysters live near the coast. Sea turtles make nests on Florida's beaches. Sailfish, red snapper, and groupers swim in the ocean.

The southern tip of Florida is a warm, semi-tropical area that attracts heat-loving animals. The endangered manatee is a mammal native to south Florida waters. Corals occupy the shallow water near the coast. These corals form the only living coral reefs in the United States.

Alligators live in Florida's wetlands. These animals have long bodies covered with scales. They are sometimes mistaken for floating logs. Adult males can grow to 11 feet (3.3 meters) and weigh up to 1,000 pounds (453 kilograms).

Wetland Issues

People have changed Florida's wetlands. They have drained more than half of the swamps and marshes for farmland. People also changed the way the water flowed. Their actions have caused flooding. Polluted water has been dumped into the wetlands.

As a result of people's actions, 16 animals in the wetlands are now in danger of disappearing. Flooding has destroyed alligator nests. The wood stork and other wading birds have decreased in numbers. Only 50 Florida panthers are alive. The American crocodile and the green turtle are also endangered.

Different groups are trying to solve the problems of the wetlands. In 1996, Florida voters decided to make polluting businesses pay for cleanup. Scientists are trying to change the way water flows. They want it to flow as it did before people drained the wetlands. In January 2002, the federal and state governments started a project to bring freshwater into the Everglades.

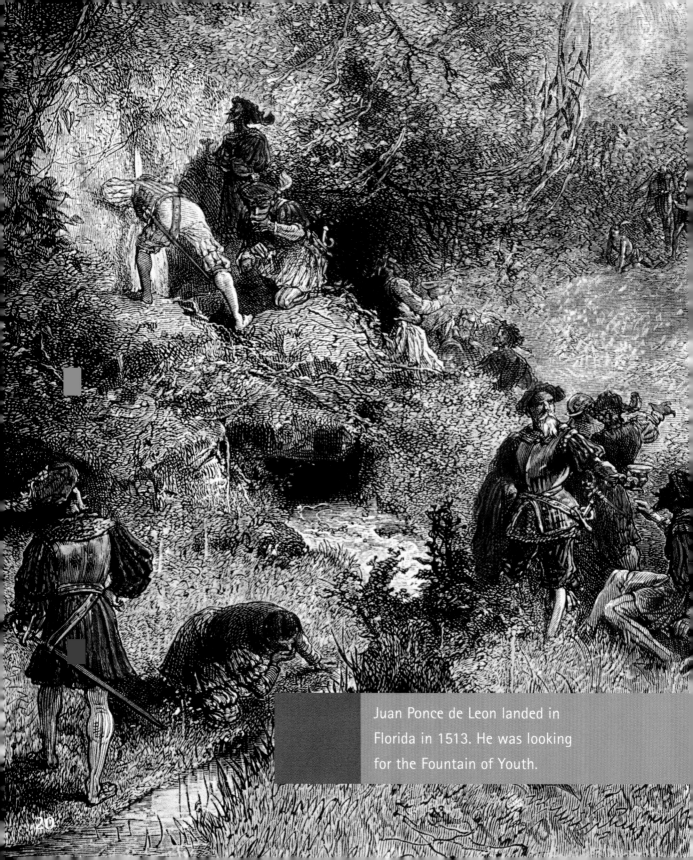

Juan Ponce de Leon landed in Florida in 1513. He was looking for the Fountain of Youth.

Chapter 3

History of Florida

When Spanish explorers arrived in the 1500s, about 25,000 American Indians lived in Florida. The Panzacola, Chatot, and Apalachicola lived in the Panhandle. The Apalachee lived just southeast of them. The northern half of the peninsula was home to the Timucua, and the southern half to the Calusa. The Matecumbe lived in the Florida Keys.

Early European Explorers

A Spanish explorer named Juan Ponce de Leon gave Florida its name. In 1513, he sailed north from Puerto Rico to look for the Fountain of Youth. He never found it, but he named the new land "La Florida," or "the Flowery Land."

In 1564, a group of French people settled near Jacksonville. Their arrival displeased the Spanish, who claimed Florida as part of Spain. King Philip II of Spain sent Pedro Menendez de Aviles to Florida to force out the French. In 1566, Menendez de Aviles built St. Augustine. This town was the first permanent European settlement in North America.

During the 1600s and 1700s, the Spanish territory spread from Georgia to the Mississippi River. The Spanish never developed a strong economy in Florida. They depended on money and food from Spanish-ruled Cuba and Mexico.

By the late 1700s, soldiers or diseases had driven away or killed most American Indians native to Florida. Pushed by arriving European settlers, Creek Indians from Georgia and Alabama moved into Florida. Florida's next European rulers, the British, called the Creeks "Seminole." This Creek word means "wild ones."

The Florida Territory

In the 1700s, European countries were settling North America. The British built colonies north of Florida. France built settlements to its west. French and British settlers fought each other in the French and Indian War (1754–1763), known in Europe as the Seven Years' War. Spain took the side of France. In 1762, the British captured Havana, Cuba. Because Spain wanted to keep the port of Havana, it agreed to give Florida to Great Britain in 1763.

Florida's Spanish rulers built St. Augustine in 1566.

23

The Seminole Indians lived in villages in the Everglades.

As the British colonies fought for independence in the Revolutionary War (1775–1783), Spain decided to take Florida back. Spain started to seek control of West Florida. The British gave West Florida back to Spain in 1781. By 1783, Spain once again had complete control of Florida.

Wars continued to be part of Florida life. U.S. General Andrew Jackson led troops into Florida in 1817. They were

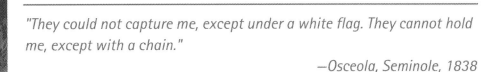

"They could not capture me, except under a white flag. They cannot hold me, except with a chain."

—Osceola, Seminole, 1838

looking for runaway slaves. The troops clashed with the Seminole who protected the runaways. Jackson's raid started the First Seminole War (1817–1818).

As U.S. troops advanced, Spain could not keep control of Florida. In 1819, Spain signed a treaty that gave Florida to the United States. Jackson governed Florida until November 1821. Congress made William P. Duval the first official governor of the new Florida Territory in 1822.

Many settlers came to Florida between 1820 and 1830. They needed land to grow cotton and other crops. They wanted the U.S. government to move the Seminole to reservations west of the Mississippi River.

The Seminole tried to keep their homes. They fought with the U.S. troops. Many Seminole were killed during the Second Seminole War (1835–1842). Most of the survivors were forced to move west.

The Third Seminole War (1855–1858) forced more of the Seminole to resettle. Only about 100 Seminole stayed in Florida by escaping into the Everglades.

Statehood and Secession

On March 3, 1845, Florida became a U.S. state. Statehood led to fast economic and population growth. The population doubled from 70,000 people in 1845 to 140,424 people in 1860. Slaves made up about 40 percent of Florida's population in 1860. Most slaves worked on cotton plantations in central Florida.

Slave labor allowed planters to grow more cotton. Planters feared that President Abraham Lincoln would end slavery. Lincoln's Republican Party was against slavery. On January 10, 1861, Florida lawmakers voted to leave the United States. It joined 10 other Southern states to form the Confederacy. Their withdrawal, or secession, from the United States pushed the country to war.

The Civil War

Florida fought on the side of the Confederacy, or South, during the Civil War (1861–1865). Florida supplied salt and cattle to the Confederate Army. While Union troops captured towns along the coast, central Florida stayed in the hands of the South. Tallahassee and Austin, Texas, were the only Confederate capitals that the Union never captured.

Many Floridians, including the men shown in this Confederate Navy yard photo, fought for the Confederacy during the Civil War.

The Union won the Civil War in 1865. The Union's victory led to the freeing of all slaves. In 1868, Florida passed a new constitution that protected African Americans' rights. Florida was allowed to rejoin the United States. But former slave owners soon gained power and wrote new laws. By 1887, the new laws had taken away most African Americans' rights.

Henry Flagler

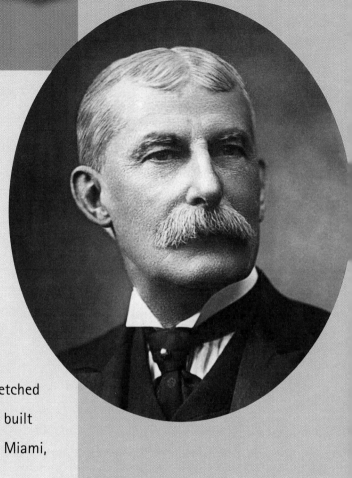

Businessman Henry Morrison Flagler (1830–1913) is one of the best known developers in Florida's history. Flagler was born in Hopewell, New York. He became a partner of the industrialist John D. Rockefeller and helped him organize the Standard Oil Company in 1870. Starting in the early 1880s, Flagler conducted most of his business activities in Florida. In 1886, he helped organize the Florida East Coast Railroad. By 1912, it stretched from Jacksonville to Key West. Flagler also built resort hotels in St. Augustine, Palm Beach, Miami, and other cities.

Developing Florida

Florida developed quickly after the Civil War. From 1860 to 1890, its population rose to nearly 270,000 people. The state government gave grants for railroads. The railroads opened up new land in central Florida and connected developed areas along the coast. They also brought tourists to the state.

People drained wetlands to create land for farms and towns. Drainage and settlement turned southern Florida into a farming region. Farmers planted orange and grapefruit trees. Ranchers in the southwest raised cattle.

The Early 1900s

In the early 1900s, the growing popularity of cars led to increased road construction. Roads made the state easier to reach.

In the 1920s, 2.5 million people moved to Florida. Most newcomers bought land near Miami. They were drawn by the warm climate and beaches. Developers built many houses and hotels.

At first, so many people wanted Florida land that it changed hands very fast. People bought land without even seeing it. Land prices rose. After a time, the prices could go no higher. Some owners found that their land was underwater. They ended up selling it at a loss.

The falling land prices caused Florida's economy to crash in 1926. Banks closed and people lost their money. Many newcomers went back north, leaving unfinished buildings behind. As the country entered the Great Depression (1929–1939), more banks failed and land values dropped even further.

Overcoming the Depression and World War II

Federal and state projects helped pull Florida out of the Great Depression. About 40,000 Floridians found jobs in public projects. Some replanted forests. Others built roads between the Florida Keys and the mainland.

Florida's economy improved in the 1940s. Tourism recovered. More citrus packing and canning houses opened. These companies shipped oranges and grapefruits to other

states. They also canned and bottled juices. Businesses started producing paper from Florida pine trees.

World War II (1939–1945) helped the economy. U.S. and British Air Force troops trained in Florida. The military bases employed Floridians.

Floridians contributed to the war effort. About 250,000 men and women served in the armed forces. Florida's location made it important in defending the United States. Thousands

Tourists came to Florida in the 1930s and 1940s to enjoy the warm weather and other attractions.

of volunteers called "spotters" kept track of airplane activity along the Florida coastline.

Post-War Development

Florida industries did well after World War II. New paper, chemical, and electronics factories opened. In 1958, Cape Canaveral became a center for space exploration.

Florida's tourist industry changed in the 1970s and 1980s. In earlier years, people had come to enjoy the beaches,

Kennedy Space Center on Cape Canaveral was the birthplace of the U.S. space program.

John F. Kennedy
Space Center
Visitor Complex

"If you can dream it, you can do it. Always remember that this whole thing was started with a dream and a mouse."
—Walt Disney, who opened Walt Disney World in Florida in 1971

wildlife, and other natural attractions. After Walt Disney World opened in 1971, tourists came to the new theme park.

Population Grows

After World War II, Florida's population grew faster than any other state. In 1930, Florida ranked 20th in population. In 2000, it ranked fourth. Mosquito control, air conditioning, and better refrigeration made life in Florida more comfortable. People from northeastern and midwestern states moved to Florida. Many retired people came to enjoy the sunshine and recreational opportunities. Immigrants from South America and the Caribbean added to the population growth.

The population growth has created challenges. The need for housing, water treatment, and sewage plants has increased. Development has destroyed natural wildlife settings. Florida officials and other groups are working hard to balance the needs of people and nature.

Florida's historic capitol stands in front of the present capitol, built in 1977.

Chapter 4

Government and Politics

At first, lawmakers from the Florida Territory met in different places. The first session was in 1822 in Pensacola in northwestern Florida. The lawmakers from St. Augustine on Florida's east coast travelled 59 days by sea to attend. The next year, the lawmakers met in St. Augustine. This time, the lawmakers from the west were shipwrecked in the passage around the peninsula. They barely escaped death.

To shorten the long, dangerous journey, the lawmakers decided to choose a halfway location for a capital city. They selected the fields of Tallahassee, then home to Seminole Indians. The legislature met in a log building in Tallahassee in 1824.

Florida's Constitutions

Florida has had several constitutions. The 1838 constitution allowed Floridians to own slaves. In 1868, Florida passed a constitution that gave African American men the right to vote. In 1883, former slave owners passed a constitution that took away this right.

Under the 1883 constitution, people had to pay a tax in order to vote. Poor people could not afford to vote. A small number of wealthy Floridians elected a large percent of the lawmakers. By 1960, 16 percent of Floridians were electing 50 percent of the legislature.

In the 1960s, the Florida civil rights movement pushed to change this system. The civil rights groups helped write a new constitution. A 1968 constitution gave voting rights to more Floridians. According to this constitution, the number of lawmakers from each area depends on how many voters live there.

The Branches of Government

The Florida state government is organized like the federal government. It includes the executive, legislative, and judicial branches.

Florida's State Government

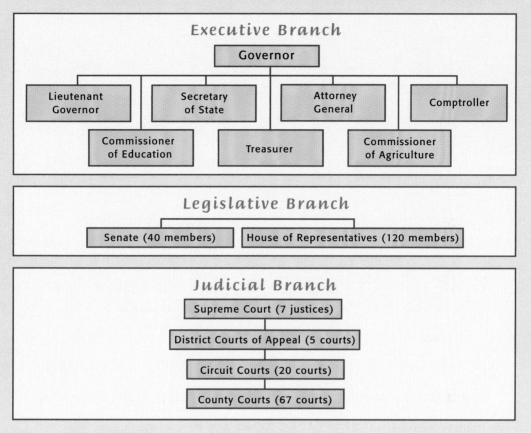

Executive Branch

Governor

- Lieutenant Governor
- Secretary of State
- Attorney General
- Comptroller
- Commissioner of Education
- Treasurer
- Commissioner of Agriculture

Legislative Branch

- Senate (40 members)
- House of Representatives (120 members)

Judicial Branch

- Supreme Court (7 justices)
- District Courts of Appeal (5 courts)
- Circuit Courts (20 courts)
- County Courts (67 courts)

The governor, lieutenant governor, and six cabinet members make up the executive branch. Unlike many states, the cabinet is elected by the people, rather than appointed by the governor.

Most Florida governors have been Democrats. Between 1845 and 2000, 33 governors were Democrats, six governors were Republicans, and four governors belonged to other parties.

The Florida legislature has two voting groups, the senate and the house of representatives. The legislature makes laws and decides how Florida tax money should be spent.

The judicial branch is the Florida court system. The highest court in the state is the Florida Supreme Court. Its seven justices are appointed by the governor. Florida has five district courts of appeal and 20 circuit courts. Each county has its own court.

Florida Makes National History

The 2000 U.S. presidential election focused attention on Florida. The election's outcome came down to Florida's results. The race between Republican George W. Bush and Democrat Al Gore was very close. Workers started to count the Florida votes on election night. At first, television stations guessed that George W. Bush was the winner. After more

Janet Reno

Floridian Janet Reno was the first woman to serve as U.S. attorney general. Reno was born on July 21, 1938, in Miami. She served as the state's attorney for Dade County near Miami for 15 years. Reno was U.S. attorney general from 1993 to 2001. She was the longest serving attorney general of the 1900s.

votes were counted, the newscasters changed their minds. The forecasts changed again and again through the night.

Finally, Bush appeared to be the winner. Gore called for a hand recount of votes in some Florida counties. Voters in those counties used punch cards to mark their choices. Some voters did not punch the holes through completely. Machines could not read their votes. Officials counted votes by hand for five weeks. In the end, the U.S. Supreme Court ended the hand count. Gore admitted defeat, and George W. Bush became president.

It's a small world

Walt Disney World in Orlando
and other attractions draw
tourists to Florida.

Chapter 5

Economy and Resources

Florida's largest industry, tourism, brings about 60 million people to the state each year. Water sports fans sail, surf, fish, or dive off the Florida coast. History lovers explore the oldest city in North America, St. Augustine. Nature lovers prefer the wilderness of the wetlands.

With its theme parks and water adventure parks, Florida is one of the world's top vacation spots. Walt Disney World in Orlando offers rides, shows, and displays. The nearby Sea World of Florida features performing killer whales, dolphins, and sea lions. Universal Studios in Orlando draws crowds with virtual adventures and live action stunts. With more than 2,700 exotic animals, Tampa's Busch Gardens offer African adventure rides, shows, and other programs.

More than half of Floridians hold tourism or other service jobs. They work in hotels, restaurants, and shops. Some dress up as characters in theme parks.

Food Industries and Farming

Florida is a major world producer of citrus fruits and juices. Only Brazil grows more oranges than Florida. One-third of the world's grapefruits come from the state.

Florida's warm climate allows crops to grow year-round. The state ships fresh and frozen fruits and vegetables to

Oranges and other citrus fruits are major farm crops in Florida.

northern states. Tomatoes are the largest vegetable crop. Florida also ships lettuce, green peppers, and celery.

Surrounded on three sides by oceans, Florida has a strong fishing industry. People catch clams, grouper, lobster, and shrimp off the coast. Ten percent of the shrimp caught each year in the United States comes from Florida.

Because of its location on the Atlantic Ocean and the Gulf of Mexico, Florida has a strong fishing industry.

Animal farms are a smaller part of Florida's agriculture. Cattle, milk, and poultry make up 20 percent of Florida's farm income. Florida farmers also raise race horses.

Manufacturing and Mining

A large part of Florida's economy is based on technology. In the 1950s, the U.S. space program began at Cape Canaveral. In 1981, the personal computer was invented in Boca Raton. Today, Florida companies make computer parts and communications equipment. Florida businesses are also known for making search and rescue equipment for the U.S. military. Florida ranks fifth in the country in the number of technology jobs.

Other types of manufacturing are also represented in the state. Florida factories make metal products, airplanes, aircraft engines, and ships. Florida's pine forests supply timber for the construction, paper, and publishing industries.

Florida's mines provide 80 percent of the phosphate rock in the United States. Phosphate is used to make fertilizer.

Cubans turned Miami into a center of Latin American banking.

Chapter 6

People and Culture

Home to nearly 16 million people, Florida is one of the fastest growing states in the nation. During the 1990s, its population rose by 3 million. Only California and Texas added more people during the 1990s.

Many ethnic traditions have shaped Florida's culture. About 65 percent of Floridians are white. Other ethnic groups are Hispanics, African Americans, and American Indians.

Cubans in Florida

About 500,000 Cubans fled to the United States after Fidel Castro took control of Cuba in 1959. Castro started a communist government that took over the land and

industries. Starting in 1965, Cubans who disagreed with Castro came to the United States on "freedom flights." In later years, they left Cuba on small boats. Some people drowned at sea, but escapes continued. Most Cubans who left settled in Florida, just 90 miles (145 kilometers) from their homeland.

Cubans are south Florida's largest community. More than 50 percent of the people in Miami are Cuban. The Cubans brought professional and business skills. They changed the region's economy and cultural life. Miami became a center of trade with Latin American countries. Its downtown did well while other U.S. inner cities lost people and businesses.

African Americans

The first African Americans in Florida were slaves who escaped into Spanish territory from British colonies. These runaways found homes with the Seminole Indians. When Florida became part of the United States, Florida's white

Florida's Ethnic Background

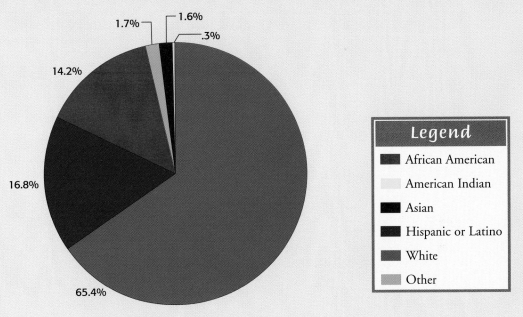

1.7% — 1.6%

.3%

14.2%

16.8%

65.4%

Legend
- African American
- American Indian
- Asian
- Hispanic or Latino
- White
- Other

settlers brought along large numbers of slaves. African Americans made up nearly half of Florida's population for most of Florida's history.

African Americans did not share equally in Florida's wealth. As late as the 1940s, they labored in camps in the Florida heartland for very low pay. Their bills for food, clothes, and lodging were bigger than their wages. They were never free of debt.

Today, African Americans are catching up with whites. African Americans still report lower incomes, but one in seven has a professional or management job. In 1992, three African Americans were elected to Congress. These lawmakers were the first black Floridians to represent their state since just after the Civil War.

American Indians

Today, about 1,500 Seminole live on five federal reservations in the state. They earn income from citrus groves, cattle, and tourism. They call themselves the "Unconquered People."

The Seminole respect the old ways. Some live in open houses made of palm trees, called chickees. The Seminole perform their dances and music at schools across Florida. They share their legends and history at the annual Florida Folk Festival.

A Retirement Destination

Florida is a favorite spot for retired people. In 2000, about 18 percent of Floridians were age 65 or older.

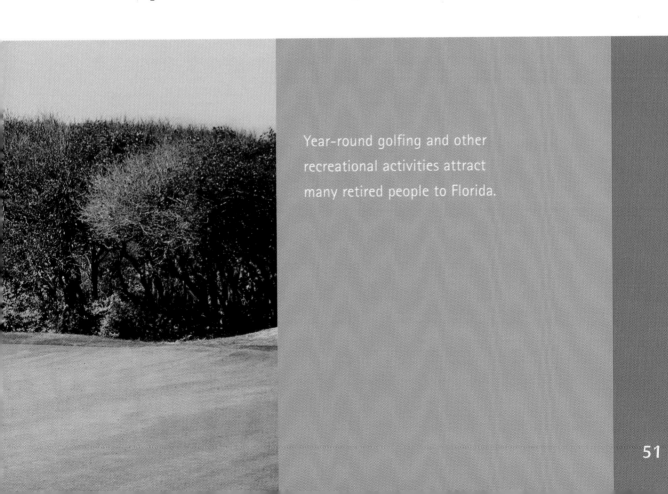

Year-round golfing and other recreational activities attract many retired people to Florida.

Older people find Florida a warm, friendly place. Housing is not very expensive, and income and inheritance taxes do not exist. Retirement villages provide care to people as they age. Retirees are also drawn by the state's many recreational and cultural activities.

A Favorite Vacation Spot

Florida is a favorite vacation spot. Its beaches are well known for their soft sand, safety, and cleanliness. Florida's waters are good locations for surfing, snorkeling, scuba diving, sailing, and fishing. People can play golf in Florida year-round.

Florida also offers a variety of museums and cultural events. Florida spends more of its budget on arts than any other state except New York. Often, museums started when wealthy people gave away their collections. For example, St. Petersburg received the world's largest private collection of works by Spanish painter Salvador Dali. The Museum of Art in Sarasota has many paintings by Peter Paul Rubens. Florida festivals celebrate jazz, modern dance, and theater.

Professional Sports

Florida sports fans cheer for a number of teams. Florida's oldest professional football team, the Miami Dolphins, has played in the Super Bowl five times. In 1997, baseball's Marlins won the World Series. Other favorites are the NBA's Miami Heat and Orlando Magic, and the NFL's Jacksonville Jaguars and Tampa Bay Buccaneers.

People worldwide see Florida as a vacation destination. But it is also a state with a rich history, natural variety, and a special blend of cultures. From citrus groves to space rockets, it is a land of inviting contrasts.

In August 2002, the Miami Dolphins played a pre-season game against the New Orleans Saints at Pro Player Stadium in Miami.

Recipe: Sunshine Shake

Florida is a major world producer of citrus fruits and juices. The recipe below uses orange and grapefruit juices, two of the state's main products.

Ingredients

1 cup (240 mL) Florida orange juice
½ cup (120 mL) Florida grapefruit juice
1 ripe banana
½ cup (120 mL) low-fat vanilla yogurt
½ teaspoon (2 mL) vanilla extract

Equipment

liquid measuring cup
measuring spoons
blender
2 glasses

What you do

1. Put all ingredients in blender. Cover and blend until smooth.

2. Pour into two glasses.

3. Serve immediately.

Makes two 8-ounce servings

Florida's Flag and Seal

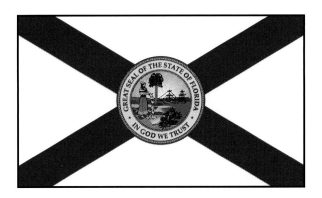

Florida's Flag

Florida's flag is white with a red X and the state seal in the center. A plain white flag with a red X was the flag of Spain in 1515. Spain was the first European country to rule Florida. The red X stands for St. Andrew, the patron saint of the Spanish region of Burgundy.

Florida's State Seal

Florida's state seal shows a Seminole woman scattering flowers. In the background are a sailboat, a palm tree, and the sun. A gold circle wraps around the seal. The words "Great Seal of the State of Florida" circle the top of the seal. The words "In God We Trust" circle the bottom.

Almanac

General Facts

Nickname: Sunshine State

Population: 15,982,378 (2000 U.S. Census)
Population rank: 4th

Capital: Tallahassee

Largest cities: Jacksonville, Miami, Tampa, Saint Petersburg, Hialeah

Agriculture

Agricultural products: citrus, vegetables, greenhouse plants, cattle, sugarcane, dairy products

Geography

Area: 65,758 square miles (170,313 square kilometers)
Size rank: 22nd

Highest point: Britton Hill, 345 feet (105 meters)

Lowest point: Atlantic and Gulf coasts, sea level

Climate

Average winter temperature: 59 degrees Fahrenheit (15 degrees Celsius)

Average summer temperature: 81 degrees Fahrenheit (27 degrees Celsius)

Average annual precipitation: 54 inches (137 centimeters)

Manatee

Sabal Palm

Natural resources: Phosphate, mineral sand deposits, forests

Types of industry: Tourism, electronics, food processing, printing and publishing, transportation equipment, machinery

Animal: Florida panther

Bird: Mockingbird

Butterfly: Zebra longwing

Freshwater fish: Largemouth bass

Flower: Orange blossom

Marine mammal: Manatee

Reptile: Alligator

Saltwater fish: Sailfish

Song: "The Swanee River" by Stephen C. Foster

Stone: Agatized coral

Tree: Sabal palm

First governor: William P. Duval

Statehood: March 3, 1845 (27th state)

U.S. Representatives: 23

U.S. Senators: 2

Electoral votes: 25

Counties: 67

Timeline

State History

1513
Spanish explorer Juan Ponce de Leon becomes the first European to see Florida.

1566
The Spanish establish St. Augustine.

1817–1858
European settlers and Seminole Indians fight three wars.

1845
On March 3, Florida becomes a state.

1861
Florida leaves the Union and joins the Confederacy.

1868
Florida rejoins the United States.

1926
Falling land prices cause Florida's economy to crash.

U.S. History

1620
Pilgrims establish a colony in the New World.

1775–1783
American colonists and the British fight in the Revolutionary War.

1861–1865
The Union and the Confederacy fight the Civil War.

1914–1918
World War I is fought; the United States enters the war in 1917.

1929–1939
The U.S. economy suffers during the Great Depression.

1941–1945
U.S. government builds World War II training camps in Florida.

1965
Freedom Flights start bringing Cubans to Miami.

1992
Hurricane Andrew hits Florida.

1958
The Kennedy Space Center opens on Cape Canaveral.

1971
Walt Disney World opens in Orlando.

2000
George W. Bush is given Florida's electoral votes and wins the U.S. presidential election.

1964
U.S. Congress passes the Civil Rights Act which outlaws discrimination.

2001
On September 11, terrorists attack the World Trade Center and the Pentagon.

1969
Neil Armstrong becomes the first man to walk on the moon.

1939–1945
World War II is fought; the United States enters the war in 1941.

Words to Know

chickee (CHIK-ee)—a Seminole home with open sides and a roof of palmetto leaves

colony (KOL-uh-nee)—an area of land settled and governed by another country

Confederacy (kuhn-FED-ur-uh-see)—the group of 11 states that declared independence from the United States before the Civil War

constitution (KON-stuh-TOO-shuhn)—an official document that explains the laws of a state and the rights of its people

dune (DOON)—a sand hill made by wind

hurricane (HUR-uh-kane)—a strong wind and rain storm that starts on the ocean

marsh (MARSH)—an area of wet, low land where grasses grow

secession (si–SESH-uhn)—the act of withdrawing from or leaving an organization; in U.S. history, secession was the withdrawal of 11 Southern states from the Union.

swamp (SWAHMP)—a wetland where trees and other plants grow

To Learn More

Chang, Perry. *Florida.* Celebrate the States. New York: Benchmark Books, 1998.

Englar, Mary. *The Seminole: The First People of Florida.* American Indian Nations. Mankato, Minn.: Bridgestone Books, 2003.

Heinrichs, Ann. *Florida.* America the Beautiful. New York: Children's Press, 1998.

Somervill, Barbara A. *Florida.* From Sea to Shining Sea. New York: Children's Press, 2001.

Internet Sites

Track down many sites about Florida.
Visit the FACT HOUND at *http://www.facthound.com*

IT IS EASY! IT IS FUN!
1) Go to *http://www.facthound.com*
2) Type in: 0736815775
3) Click on "FETCH IT" and FACT HOUND will find several links hand-picked by our editors.

Relax and let our pal FACT HOUND do the research for you!

Places to Write and Visit

Everglades National Park
40001 State Road 9336
Homestead, FL 33034-6733

Florida Museum of Natural History
P.O. Box 112710
34th Street and Hull Road
University of Florida (Powell Hall)
Gainesville, FL 32611-2710

Governor's Office
PL 05 The Capitol
400 South Monroe Street
Tallahassee, FL 32399-0001

Kennedy Space Center Visitor Complex
State Road 405
Mail Code: DNPS
Kennedy Space Center, FL 32899

Museum of Florida History
500 South Bronough Street
Tallahassee, FL   32399-0250

Plants bloom in the Big Cyprus Swamp in southern Florida.

Index